Whale Life

Funny & Weird

Marine Mammals

Funny & Weird Animals Series

By

P. T. Hersom

Whale Life Funny & Weird Marine Mammals

By P. T. Hersom

First Published, 2013

Printed in the United States of America

Hersom House Publishing

3365 NE 45th St, Suite 101

Ocala, Florida 34479 USA

Whales are Marine Mammals

Marine mammals are animals that breathe air, live in the water, give live birth as opposed to laying eggs, nurse their young, and are warm blooded. Whales, dolphins, seals, sea lions, porpoises, manatees, sea otters and even polar bears are marine mammals.

Whales have hair! What? Yes, every mammal has hair even marine mammals! For many marine mammals like seals, polar bears and sea lions, their hair creates a warm insulation to protect them from cold water and air. Whales, dolphins and porpoises only have hair on their faces and many lose their hair shortly after being born.

Many marine mammals have a thick layer of fat on their body called blubber, which stores energy and keeps them warm. Most spend their entire life in the water, but some spend more time on land. Whales, dolphins and manatees have to stay in the water. However, seals, walruses, otters and polar bears come out of the water to eat, lie in the sun, to mate and give birth.

Scientists group marine mammals into four different groups: Cetaceans, Pinnipeds, Sirenians and Fissipeds.

Cetaceans – consist of whales, dolphins and porpoises, which completely spend their life in the water.

Pinnipeds – meaning fin-footed, such as walruses, sea lions and seals have four fins or flippers, two in the back and two in the front. They spend most of their time in the water, but go to land to breed.

Sirenians – also known as sea cows, like the manatee and dugong they have two arms and a paddle shaped tail. They spend all of their life in the water and never go to land.

Fissipeds – have separate digits, meaning fingers, thumbs and toes, such as the polar bear and otter. The polar bear spend most of their time on land and go to the water for food.

Whale Life

Whales live in family groups called pods ranging from 2 to 30 whales. Some pods though, can grow to more than 100's of individuals during migration periods. The daddy whale is called a bull, the mommy whale is called a cow, and baby whales are called calves. Unlike people, whale calves are born fin (feet) first. This helps keep them from drowning during the birth process. Calves will nurse from their mother for at least 12 months before eating on their own. The whale cow's milk is high in fat content, so rich that it has the consistency of toothpaste! Calves form a strong bond with their mothers.

There are over 20 different kinds of whales with many varied colors, shapes and sizes. Some whales are only 11 ft/3.5 m long, while others grow to over 110 ft/33.6 m in length. They breathe through a blowhole located on top of their head. The whale tail is called a fluke and their side fins are called flippers. Most whales have dorsal fins on their back, but not all do.

Whales live longer than most animals, on average most species live from 25 to 50 years. However, the Humpback is estimated to live up to 77 years and in 2007 a Bowhead near Alaska was found to have a 19th century lance fragment in its body. Indicating it was between 115 and 130 years old! Now that's older than my Great Grandpa. How about yours?

It can be hard to tell the bull (male) whales from the cow (female) whales because when not in use the bull's genitals or private parts, are tucked away inside of a cavity allowing the bull to swim faster.

Whales are intelligent social mammals that communicate with each other through vocal clicks, groans, moans, whistles and melodic sounds. Some whales even sound like they are singing, it's called whale songs. In captivity some whales have been known to mimic human speech. Scientists find this amazing since the whale vocal mechanism is so different than humans. Now that would be weird to hear.

Whale watching has become popular worldwide and whales can put on a good show for the spectators. By breaching, this is jumping high out of the water, tail slapping, flipper waving, spy- hopping, which is when the whale rises and holds its head out of the water, and lobtailing, this is when they stick their fluke (tail) out of the water, swing it around and then slap it hard on the surface.

Whales are different from other animals in the fact that they are not conscious breathers. So when it's time for bed, whales sleep with one part of their brain awake and the other in slow-wave sleep mode. This allows them to stay awake just enough to watch for predators and keep their blowholes above water to breathe. Weird. Instead of sleep walking would you call this sleep swimming?

Tooth or Baleen?

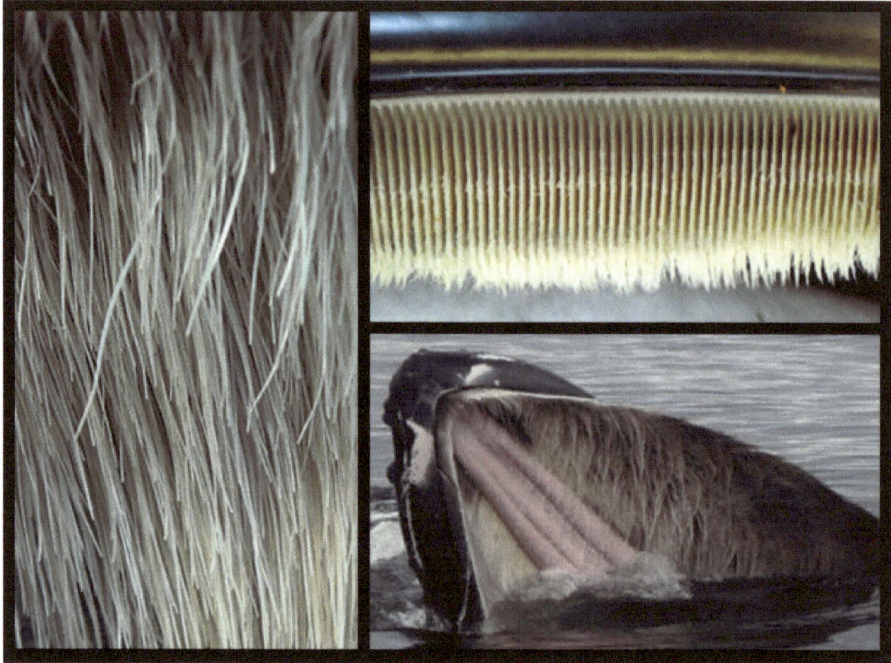

All whales either have teeth or baleen. Now the ones with teeth, of course eat with their teeth, and the ones with baleen eat with... What's that? Oh, what is baleen? Well baleen is a row of large plates made of keratin attached to the upper jaw. These baleen plates are made of the same stuff as our hair and fingernails. Connected to each plate are tiny hairs which form a filter system.

Whales with baleen are called baleen whales. This type of whale feeds by eating huge amounts of small organisms at a time, like an ocean vacuum cleaner. The whale will find a large group of prey such as krill or zooplankton, and then with mouth wide open swim through it. Then filter the water from the food through the baleen plates.

Baleen whales have other features that are different from toothed whales too, such as, two blowholes instead of one. They're larger than toothed whales and baleen cows are generally bigger than the bulls.

Now, you would think toothed whales chew prey with their teeth, but that's not true. I know it's kind of weird. They actually swallow their prey whole, unless it is too big to swallow with one gulp. In that case, they will tear off chunks and then swallow the smaller chunks whole.

Tooth whales find food through echolocation. Echolocation is when the whale makes clicking sounds that travel underwater until they hit their prey, then bounces back revealing the location, shape and size. Tooth whales are faster swimmers than the baleens and always have at least one dorsal fin.

Harpoons Away!

Since the 17th century whales have been hunted for their meat, whale oil, baleen and ambergris which were used in many perfumes. In its glory day of the mid 1800's, the American whaling industry had 736 ships and employed over 70,000 workers. More than 2 million whales were killed during the 20th century and by mid century many whales were almost driven into extinction.

Because of this, in 1946 the International Whaling Commission was formed to monitor the falling whale populations and the whaling industry. In 1986 most countries agreed to ban commercial whaling. Currently only the countries of Japan, Iceland and Norway have active whaling and some native communities are allowed to take whales for food in Alaska, northern Canada and Siberia.

Now let's see some funny & weird whales.

Beluga Whale

Size: Up to 18 ft/5.5m in length and weigh 3,500 lb/1,600 kg.

Where they live: In the Arctic and sub-Arctic oceans around worldwide.

Tell Me More

The Beluga is also called the White Whale or Melonhead for obvious reasons or Sea Canary because of its high pitched vocal sounds. This cutie is popular among visitors of marine themed parks throughout the world because of their unique white color and their funny personalities.

They are part of the toothed whales and like to eat fish, shrimp, octopus and crustaceans found on the seabed around 1,000 ft/300 m deep. Besides their white color and paddle like fins, Belugas have no dorsal fin on their back and that makes them different from their whale cousins.

Belugas are social mammals forming pods of 3 to 25 whales, and most migrate in the summer months to join up with other pods in coastal rivers, bays and shallow areas. This is the time cows will give birth to new calves. The baby calve will be nursed by its mother until its almost 2 years old. Then it will start to eat small fish and shrimp.

They are very vocal using high pitched squeals, whistles, clicks and squeaks to talk to one another. Their sounds travel through water four times faster than sound does through air!

Some researchers claim to have taught Belugas to talk with people by identifying different things with different sounds. In the wild, Belugas have been reported to make sounds that "sound like" human voices. Now that's weird. Would you talk to one if it talked to you?

Blue Whale

Size: Up to 110 ft/33.6 m in length and weigh 190 tons/170 tonnes.

Where they live: In the Pacific, Atlantic and Indian Oceans.

Tell Me More

The Blue Whale is the largest animal ever to have existed in the world! Their hearts are so big; they can weigh as much as a car and their tongues have a similar weight as a bull elephant! Their flippers grow up to 13 ft/4 m long. So you can imagine it takes a lot of food to fuel that big body. They eat on average 4.4 tons/4 tonnes of krill per day. Now that's a big appetite.

With their long slender shape, Blue Whales can reach speeds of 31 mph/50 km/h over short bursts. Even though too low for us to hear, they are one of the loudest creatures on earth, talking to one another using a series of low frequency pulses, clicks and groans.

Although deep water hunters, Blue Whales must come to the surface to breathe. Breathing through twin blowholes as pictured above, the whale emits a fantastic spout up to 39 ft/12 m high into the air!

Blue Whales mate in late autumn through the winter, although not much is known about their mating behavior. The cows mate once every two to three years giving birth to one calve.

After a Blue Whale calf is born, it will drink around 110 gal/400 l of milk every day, and nurses until 7 months old. The calves gain weight fast, as much as 200 lb/90 kg on average every day. Even at birth they weigh as much as a hippopotamus!

Bowhead Whale

Size: Up to 66 ft/20 m and weigh 110 tons/100 tonnes.

Where they live: In Arctic and sub-Arctic waters worldwide.

Tell Me More

The Bowhead Whale was named after the shape of its mouth, which looks like a bow of a boat or ship. They have very thick blubber, growing up to 1.5 ft/.5 m thick which keeps them warm in the cold Arctic water. They have a wide fluke which can be up to 25 ft/7.5 m across. Like the Beluga Whale they lack a dorsal fin and usually are seen on the surface as two bumps, only having their head and back being exposed.

Their baleen grows the longest of any whale up to 10 ft/3 m in length. That's truly a mouth full. Capturing food from the surface and the sea floor, they can hold their breath up to 40 minutes.

Fin Whale

Size: Up to 89.5 ft/27 m and weigh 82 tons/74 tonnes.

Where they live: In polar and tropical oceans worldwide.

Tell Me More

The Fin Whale is a long slender whale, and the second longest animal in the world. They are fast swimmers able to swim 23 mph/37 km/h, which earned them the nickname "Greyhounds of the Sea". They migrate in the winter to warmer subtropical waters and in the summer they swim to northern cooler waters to feed.

They make a variety of sounds when they are feeding and talking, like moans, grunts, and pulse sounds. These sounds can last for over 15 minutes at a time. Scientists have proven the sounds can travel over 100 miles/161 km, and possibly thousands of miles/km away.

Gray Whale

Size: Up to 50 ft/15 m and weigh 40 tons/36 tonnes.

Where they live: In the North Pacific Ocean.

Tell Me More

The Gray Whale is a light gray color and has encrusted patches of barnacles and whale lice that are dark gray and white. They are another whale that lacks a dorsal fin on their back.

Known for their long migration, Grey Whales will travel over 14,000 miles/22,000 km during their roundtrip migration. Starting in October, they swim from the northern Pacific down the coast of

California to the Baja Peninsula of Mexico averaging 75 miles/120 km a day. By January they can be seen from shore between the area of Monterey and San Diego, California and have become a favorite of whale watchers.

The whales will head for the protection of the shallow lagoons of Baja where the cows will give birth to new calves. These shallow waters ward off Killer Whales and sharks from attacking the calves, which at birth can be 13 ft/4 m long and weigh 1,100 lb/500 kg. That's a big baby. Calves will drink 300 gal/1,100 l of their mother's milk a day, which is made of 53% fat. What happened to low fat or at least 2% milk?

The Gray Whales are friendly and don't seem to mind being the star attraction of whale watching tours. In the picture above you can see a calf interacting with people and even allowing a friendly kiss.

Gray Whales are bottom feeders. I mean "real" bottom feeders. They scoop up sediment from the ocean floor with their large mouth. This sediment contains sand, water, little sea animals and crustaceans such as amphipods. Then using their baleen plates they filter out the sediment, sand and water, leaving only the creatures.

Humpback Whale

Size: Up to 52 ft/16 m and weigh 39 tons/35 tonnes.

Where they live: In seas and ocean waters worldwide.

Tell Me More

The Humpback Whale is a favorite among whale watchers due to its acrobatic breaching and slapping the water's surface with its pectoral fins and tail. They are easily recognized from other whales by the hump on its back and the large fins which grow to almost one third of the body length. The Humpback is covered with grey to black coloring and white markings on its underside. Differing in each whale, the white markings are like fingerprints allowing scientist to recognize individual whales.

They make the longest migration of whales, each year covering over 16,000 miles/25,000 km.

One funny fact about the Humpback is that they ONLY eat in the summer! During the summer months they eat their fill of krill and small fish while in the northern polar waters. Then in the winter they migrate to subtropical and tropical waters to mate and give birth to new calves. During this time they do not eat and only live off the stored fat built up in their blubber.

Shown in the picture above are Humpback Whales applying their special feeding method called "bubble net feeding". They do this by swimming in a shrinking circle blowing bubbles underneath a school of prey, ever shrinking the ring of bubbles around the prey until it confines them into a smaller column trapped within the bubbles.

This may take dozens of whales working together blowing bubbles, some whales diving deeper to push the prey towards the top, and others using sounds to herd the fish into the bubble net. When the circle gets smaller the whales plunge through the bubble net with their mouths wide open, swallowing thousands of fish in one big bite!

What will you think about the next time you blow bubbles? Hopefully, not in the bathtub.

Humpbacks make several funny and weird vocal sounds like snorts, groans, grunts and even barks! The bull humpbacks can sing and are known for their long, loud whale songs which can last up to 20 minutes. Since they have no vocal cords like people do, they push air through their large nose cavities to make their song notes, sometimes singing for more than a whole day.

Humpbacks are playful and known for their breaching, but they are also known for tail waving called "lobtailing". This is when they stick their fluke (tail) out of the water, swing it around and then slap it hard on the surface. This makes a very loud noise and can be heard miles/kilometers away.

Killer Whale or Orca

Size: Up to 32 ft/9.7 m in length and weigh 12,000 lb/5,443 kg.

Where they live: In all oceans throughout the world.

Tell Me More

The killer Whale is not a whale, but the largest member in the dolphin family. They are one of the most powerful predators on earth and an apex predator, meaning it has no natural enemy. They dive down to 1,000 ft/305 m when looking for food. That's a long way to hold your breath!

Killer Whales are also known by the name Orca. Like other dolphins they feed on fish, plus much larger prey like seals, sharks and whales. Hunting together in groups or packs similar to what wolfs do, they are sometimes called "The Wolves of the Sea".

Killer Whales are intelligent predators and are known for "spyhopping", which is when the whale holds its head above water and looks around for prey, such as penguins standing on top of ice floes. Working together several Killer Whales will form a line and swim swiftly towards the ice floes. A line of whales push a lot of water and just before impact they turn away and the water surges over the ice, backwashing the penguins into the sea.

Killer Whales have the second largest brain of any marine mammal. Being very social they use whistles, clicks and even a variety of screams to communicate with each other. Have you ever screamed to communicate with someone? Scientists have noticed that some pods even have their own language.

Minke Whale

Size: Up to 35 ft/11 m in length and weigh 5.5 tons/5 tonnes.

Where they live: In sub Antarctic and Antarctic Ocean waters.

Tell Me More

The Minke Whale is the second smallest baleen whale in the world, only the Pygmy Right Whale is smaller. They are easily identified by the white band on each flipper, which stands out against their dark grey back.

They are one of the most abundant whales on earth and have been given the nickname Stinky Minkes by whale watchers. This is because they are often seen, but do not breach or raise their flukes out of the water, and can stay underwater for 20 minutes at a time.

Narwhal Whale

Size: Without tusk up to 18 ft/5.5 m in length and weigh 3,500 lb/1,600 kg.

Where they live: In Arctic and Atlantic Oceans.

Tell Me More

Truly the unicorn of the sea, the male Narwhal Whale has a long single tusk, or canine tooth that grows from the left side of the upper mouth, twisting as it grows through the lip! This tusk can grow up to 10 ft/3.1 m long, and though it has a scary look to it, it's hollow and only weighs about 22 lb/10 kg.

Though it's a rare occurrence, some will grow a second tusk with the right canine tooth. Only about 15% of female Narwhals will ever grow tusks. In medieval times, the washed ashore Narwhal tusks were thought to be from a mythical unicorn horse.

Their tusks grow rapidly during their youth and are thought to play a role during the mating season. Some have been found with broken tusks which point to fighting and others have been seen crossing tusks as if they were sword fighting. This is called tusking, "On Guard" Narwhal.

They live in the Greenlandic and Canadian Arctic waters and rarely are seen far from the ice. They dive up to 5,000 ft/1524 m deep in search of food; this is very deep for a marine mammal. During these dives they will hold their breath up to 25 minutes. How long can you hold your breath?

Pilot Whale

Size: Up to 24 ft/7.2 m in length and weigh 7,055 lb/3200 kg.

Where they live: In oceans worldwide.

Tell Me More

Pilot Whales are actually dolphins, and not whales. They're the second largest dolphin and sometimes called blackfish due to their black coloring. They can dive to deep depths of 2,000 ft/610 m and hold their breath up to 16 minutes before coming back to the surface. They have been nicknamed "Cheetahs of the Deep" because of their fast swimming ability in deep water.

They have a high level of social activity and talk with different sounds such as whistles, squeals, clicks, snores and whining. I know some people talk by whining, but not by snoring? Now that's funny!

Pygmy Sperm Whale

Size: Up to 11 ft/ 3.5 m in length and weigh 880 lb/400 kg.

Where they live: In tropical and temperate waters of the Pacific, Indian and Atlantic Oceans.

Tell Me More

The Pygmy Sperm Whale is the smallest whale in the world. These little guys are rarely spotted at sea and so little is known about them except from when they are beached whales. As seen in the picture above, a team of marine scientists attempt a whale rescue of a beached Pygmy Sperm Whale.

They are known in Japan as the Floating Whale because of its behavior to slowly rise to the surface with little blow or splash and then just stay their motionless for long periods of time. They tend to be shy and stay away from boats and on a rare moment may be seen breaching.

Right Whale

Size: Up to 59 ft/18 m in length and weigh 100 tons/91 tonnes.

Where they live: In the North Atlantic and North Pacific Oceans and waters of the Southern Hemisphere.

Tell Me More

Right Whales are large round whales that grow larger than the Gray and Humpback Whales, but smaller than the Blue Whale. They have noticeable rough, white colored patches of skin on its head that is caused by whale lice. Weird! They are hairier than most whales, with around 100 on the upper jaw and approximately 300 found on the lower, funny.

Hunted nearly into extinction, the Right Whale is now the most endangered in the world.

Their large size, friendly slow nature and coastal habitat, all contributed to making them an easy catch for whalers. In addition, once killed they would float and have a rich source of blubber and oil.

They feed by skimming across the water's surface with their mouth wide open, scooping up the krill, crustaceans and zooplankton. As with other baleen whales they filter out the water and sediment from their captured lunch with large baleen plates. The Right Whales baleen plates grow to 8 ft/2.4 m in length. When feeding, the water flowing across their baleen plates creates a clicking sound called a "baleen rattle."

Right Whales are slow swimmers, however; very acrobatic and often breach, lobtail and tail slap the water. Also displaying their unique V-shaped blow, caused from their two widely spaced blowholes, shoots water to heights of 16 ft/5 m into the air making them a favorite of whale watchers worldwide.

Sperm Whale

Size: Up to 67 ft/20.5 m in length and weigh 63 tons/57 tonnes.

Where they live: Worldwide in all oceans.

Tell Me More

Sperm Whales have the biggest head of any animal on earth. It ranges to 10 ft/3 m high, by 7 ft/2.1 m wide, by 20 ft/6 m in length making up one third of the whales entire body length! As you can see in the picture, they usually have scars around their head made from giant squid attacks. Giant squid is the whale's favorite thing to eat off the deep diving takeout menu.

They produce ambergris, a waste product of its digestive system, and sometimes contain squid beaks. Scientists think it may help protect the sperm whale from the stings of the giant squid, its favorite food. Huge lumps of ambergris are sometimes found vomited up by the whale, yuck!

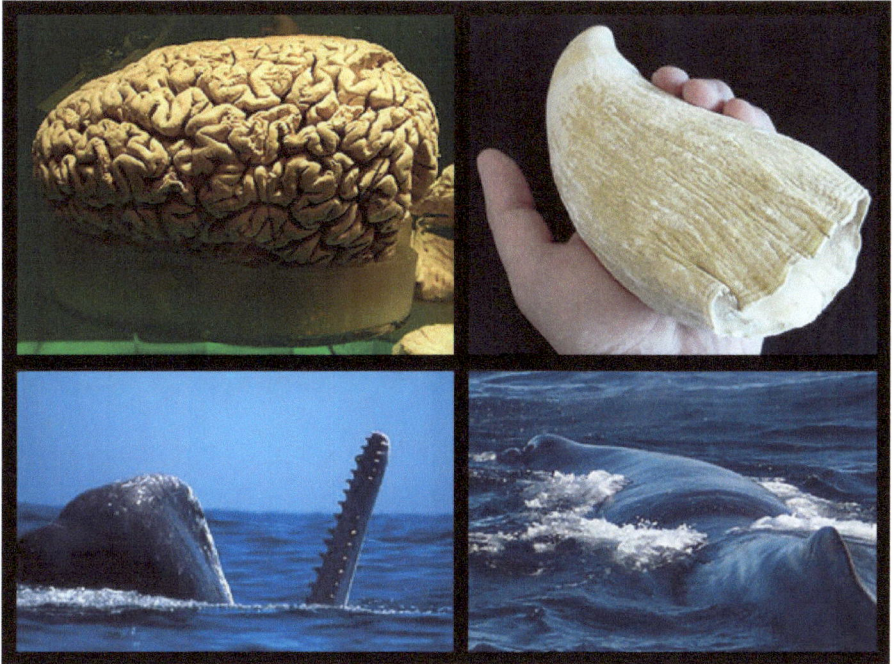

The Sperm Whale has the largest brain on earth weighing about 20 lb/9 kg and is the largest of the toothed whales. They only have teeth on their lower jaw which fits into sockets of the upper jaw. These teeth weigh around 2.2 lb/1 kg each. With a tooth that big I'm sure when they get a cavity it really hurts. Stay away from the sweets.

They have a very distinctive S shaped blowhole that is located in the front of their head and shifted to the left side. This causes their blow spray to shoot forward and wide.

The whales can dive to almost 2 miles/3.2 km deep in search of giant squid to eat, which makes them the deepest diving whale. On these deep dives they may stay submerged for 90 minutes! An average adult Sperm Whale will eat 1 tons/.9 tonnes of food per day. That's one hungry whale.

Sperm Whales eat more than just giant squid. In addition, they eat rays, octopuses and even the huge colossal squid. Three Sperm Whales were one time observed attacking a mammoth plankton eating Megamouth Shark.

Sperm Whales are often observed "logging". Logging is when they lie motionless at the water's surface, resting with their fluke hanging down. While floating like this, part of the head, dorsal fin and parts of the back are exposed above the surface. In this state they are easily spotted and approached.

When Sperm Whales go to sleep, they position themselves into a vertical, or up and down position with their head just below or at the water's surface. They sleep in short periods of time, about 7% of the day. Recently scientists have discovered that unlike other whales, they may sleep with both sides of their brain at the same time, generally between 9 p.m. and midnight.

They use clicking sounds called echolocation to communicate and to find food in dark deep waters. Also, Sperm Whale cows keep track of their young calf when diving for prey since the calf cannot dive as deep because they need to breathe more often. Their vocal sounds are the loudest in the world, up to 230 decibels. The loudest jet airliner taking off is only 150 decibels!

Moby Dick

In the classic novel "Moby Dick", the notorious whale in the story was an albino Sperm Whale, like the one pictured above. The 1851 novel by Herman Melville was inspired by true events. The American whaleship Essex, from Nantucket, Massachusetts, was attacked and sunk by a huge Sperm Whale in the southern Pacific Ocean, in the year 1820. The following is a quote from Owen Chase, the First Mate of the Essex during the attack.

"I turned around and saw him about one hundred rods [500 m or 550 yards] directly ahead of us, coming down with twice his ordinary speed of around 24 knots/44 km/h, and it appeared with tenfold fury and vengeance in his aspect. The surf flew in all

directions about him with the continual violent thrashing of his tail. His head about half out of the water, and in that way he came upon us, and again struck the ship." —Owen Chase.

The Nantucket Whaling Museum has an 18 ft/5.5 m long jawbone claiming to be from an 80 ft/24 m long Sperm Whale. *Moby Dick was claimed to be 85 ft/26 m in length, whoa!*

What Did You Learn Today? Questions

1. The Beluga Whale can talk with people, true or false?

2. Are Blue Whales the smallest whale in the world?

3. I have the longest baleen of any whale growing up to 10 ft/3 m? What is my name?

4. The Fin Whale's vocal sounds can be heard over 100 miles/161 km away, true or false?

5. Gray Whale calves can drink 300 gal/1,100 l of milk in one day, true or false?

6. During migration the Humpback will travel 16,000 miles/25,000 km, true or false?

7. Is the Killer Whale really a dolphin?

8. Whale watchers nicknamed me Stinky Minke. What is my real name?

9. Narwhal Whales like to sword fight, true or false?

10. Pilot Whales can fly over the water, true or false?

11. In Japan they call me the Floating Whale, but most of the time you can find me beached? Who am I?

12. The Right Whale has hair, true or false?

13. When Sperm Whales order takeout for lunch, what do they get?

14. The book Moby Dick was based on a true story, true or false?

What Did You Learn Today? Answers

1) True, of course they do not talk like people do, but they have been trained to talk with people by identifying different things with different sounds.

2) No, they are the largest whale, and animal in the world.

3) The Bowhead Whale.

4) True.

5) True.

6) True, they have the longest migration of any whale.

7) Yes, it is the largest of the dolphin family.

8) The Minke Whale.

9) True! It is called tusking.

10) False.

11) The Pygmy Sperm Whale.

12) True.

13) Giant Squid.

14) True.

Other Books to Enjoy by P. T. Hersom

Available at - amzn.to/18qcwjB

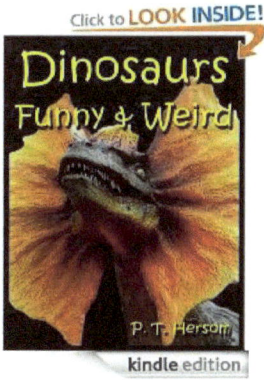

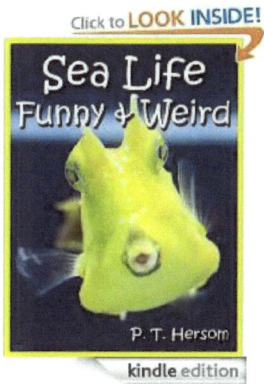

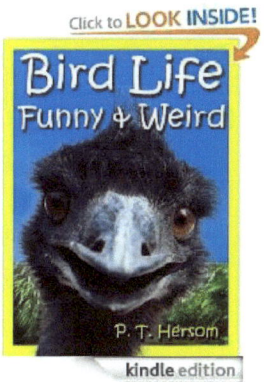

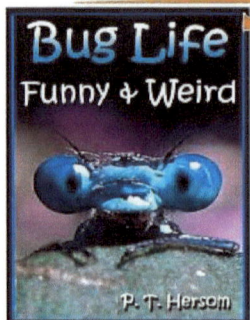

Click to LOOK INSIDE!

Bug Life
Funny & Weird

P. T. Hersom

kindle edition

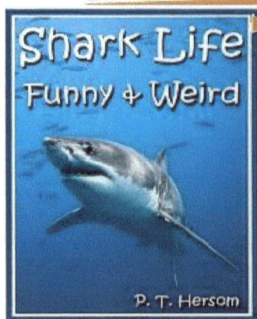

Click to LOOK INSIDE!

Shark Life
Funny & Weird

P. T. Hersom

kindle edition

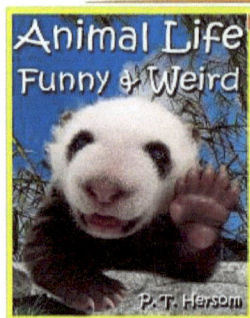

Click to LOOK INSIDE!

Animal Life
Funny & Weird

P. T. Hersom

kindle edition

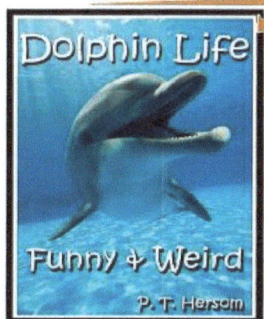

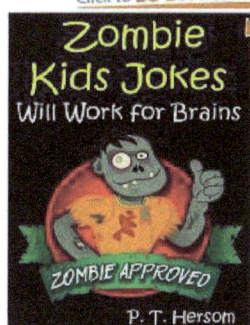

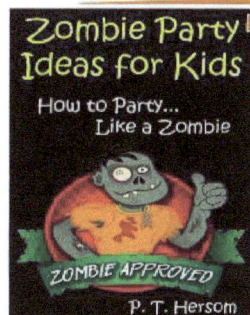

Dolphin Life

Funny & Weird

P. T. Hersom

kindle edition

Zombie
Kids Jokes
Will Work for Brains

ZOMBIE APPROVED

P. T. Hersom

kindle edition

Zombie Party
Ideas for Kids

How to Party...
Like a Zombie

ZOMBIE APPROVED

P. T. Hersom

kindle edition

Enjoyed the Book?

Thank you for buying this book. I hope that you and your children enjoy reading the book and learning about the animals in the book as much as I did writing it. If you found the book enjoyable, please help me out by posting a review on the Amazon page. Thank you for taking the time to do so. It is very much appreciated.

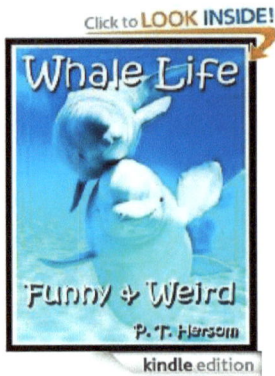

www.ingramcontent.com/pod-product-compliance
Lightning Source LLC
Chambersburg PA
CBHW041359090426
42741CB00001B/16